Introduction to Academic Writing

THIRD EDITION

Answer Key

Alice Oshima
Ann Hogue

PEARSON
Longman

Introduction to Academic Writing, Third Edition
Answer Key

Pearson Education, 10 Bank Street, White Plains, NY 10606

Staff credits: The people who made up the *Introduction to Academic Writing, Third Edition, Answer Key* team,
representing editorial, production, design, and manufacturing, are: Rhea Banker, Wendy Campbell, Elizabeth Carlson,
Gina DiLillo, Christine Edmonds, Laura Le Dréan, Linda Moser, Edith Pullman, and Paula Van Ells.

Text composition: Integra
Text font: Times 11.5/14.5

ISBN: 0-13-241028-1

Printed in the United States of America
5 6 7 8 9 10—OPM—11 10 09 08

Contents

Chapter 1: Paragraph Format

Capitalization (page 6)

2. English 001—name of a school course with a number
3. April—month
4. Introducing Myself—title
5. Hello—first word in a sentence
6. I—pronoun
7. El Salvador—place on a map
8. San Salvador—place on a map
9. United States—place on a map
10. New York—place on a map
11. Uncle Eduardo—title and name of a person
12. Brooklyn—place on a map
13. City College—name of a school
14. English—name of a language
15. Spanish—name of a language

Practice 1: Capitalization (pages 8–9)

A.
2. Her major is business.
3. Thanksgiving is a holiday in both Canada and the United States, but it is celebrated on different days in the two countries.
4. It is celebrated on the fourth Thursday in November in the United States and on the second Monday in October in Canada.
5. Istanbul is a seaport city in Turkey.
6. Greenhills College is located in Boston, Massachusetts.
7. I am taking four classes this semester: American history, Sociology 32, Economics 40, and a computer science course.
8. I read a good book last weekend by Ernest Hemingway called *The Old Man and the Sea*.
9. My roommate is from the South, so she speaks English with a southern accent.
10. The two main religions in Japan are Buddhism and Shintoism.

B. Editing Practice

A Future Businessman

I would like to introduce my classmate Roberto Sanchez. He is from the beautiful island of Puerto Rico in the Caribbean Sea. Roberto is twenty-one years old. He was born in San Juan, the capital city. His native language is Spanish. He studied English in elementary school and in high school, too. Roberto comes from a large family. He has three older brothers and two younger sisters. He likes to play the electric bass. He and some friends have a small band. Sometimes they play on Saturday nights at the Fantasia Club on Fourth Street in downtown San Jose. Baseball is his favorite sport. The San Francisco Giants are his favorite team. Now he is studying English at

Greenhills College. In September of next year, he will begin to study business and computer science at a university. After graduation, he wants to work for a large tech company such as Intel or IBM.

Questions on the Model (page 10)
1. Subject: Filmmaker George Lucas. Verb: has changed.
2. Subject: Lucas. 2 verbs: studied, made.
3. Verb: have transformed. 2 subjects: love of story telling (and) technological innovations.

Practice 2: Identifying Subjects, Verbs, and Prepositional Phrases (page 13)
3. I am a student (at Greenhills College) (in Boston, Massachusetts).
4. Some (of my classes) are difficult.
5. Some (of the homework) is boring.
6. A lot (of my classes) are in Dante Hall.
7. A lot (of my time) is spent (in the student lounge).
8. My father works (in an office).
9. None (of my brothers) are married.
10. None (of the money) was stolen.
11. My youngest brother and sister are still (in high school).
12. My father understands English but doesn't speak it.
13. (In South America) most (of the people) are Catholic.
14. Neither (of my parents) has been (to the United States).

Practice 3: Subject-Verb Agreement (pages 13–14)

A.
              s
2. Some of the teachers (speak/~~speaks~~) my language.

             s
3. Each of the gifts (was/~~were~~) carefully wrapped in gold paper.

             s
4. One of the words on the test (was/~~were~~) misspelled.

             s
5. A lot of my classes (~~was~~/were) cancelled last week.

             s
6. A lot of my time (is/~~are~~) spent in the library.

               s
7. In my country most of the people (want to go/~~wants to go~~) to college.

              s
8. (~~Do~~/Does) anyone know the correct time?

              s
9. There (~~is~~/are) several kinds of flowers in the bouquet.

10. There (wasn't/~~weren't~~) <u>any electricity</u> in our building last night.
    <small>s</small>

11. <u>The noise</u> from the firecrackers (was/~~were~~) loud.
    <small>s</small>

B. Editing Practice

Young Golf Stars

¹Golf is no longer the sport of rich, middle-aged, white men. ²Young people around the world <u>are</u> taking up the game, and some of them <u>are</u> taking it over. ³One of the young stars <u>is</u> Sergio Garcia, a fascinating young golfer from Spain. ⁴Sergio was born in 1980 and started playing golf at the age of three. ⁵He became a professional golfer in 1999 at the age of nineteen. ⁶Sergio became famous by hitting a golf shot at a target from behind a tree with his eyes closed. ⁷Two other young golf stars are Tiger Woods and Michelle Wie. ⁸Both Tiger and Michelle started playing golf at very young ages, and both <u>have</u> ethnic backgrounds. ⁹Tiger, born in California in 1975, is Thai-African-American-Native American. ¹⁰Michelle, born in Hawaii in 1989, is Korean-American. ¹¹Each of these two young Americans <u>has</u> shocked the world of golf in different ways. ¹²Tiger shocked everyone by becoming the best golfer in the world while still in his early twenties. ¹³Michelle shocked everyone by competing against men—and beating many of them—at the age of fourteen. ¹⁴It is clear that all three of these young golfers <u>have</u> great futures ahead of them.

Practice 4: Fragments (page 15)

A. <u>X</u> 2. Jose and Jin ‸the smartest students in the class.
    <small>are</small>

<u>X</u> 4. The baby ‸finally sleepy.
    <small>is</small>

<u>X</u> 6. Ms. Woodbury, our grammar teacher, ‸often late on Fridays.
    <small>is</small>

<u>X</u> 7. ‸~~Is~~ important for students to get to class on time.
    <small>It is</small>

B. Editing Practice

My Best Friend

My best friend is Suzanne. We have been friends since childhood. As children we lived next door to each other in Caracas. Now <u>we</u> live in different countries on different continents. She is married to a Venezuelan. <u>She</u> has three children. Her son <u>is</u> two years old, and her twin daughters <u>are</u> three months old. We haven't seen each other for eight years. We keep in touch by e-mail. <u>We</u> also telephone each other at least once a month. We will be friends forever.

Chapter 2: Narrative Paragraphs

Questions on the Model (page 24)
1. Sentences 1, 5, 9, and 15.
2. Suddenly, At first, Then, Meanwhile, At last, Then, Next.

Practice 1: Time Order (pages 25–28)
A. Words and phrases to add: Suddenly, At first, Then.
B. *Note*: There is more than one possible way to complete this exercise.

Thanksgiving

Thanksgiving in the United States is a day for families to be together and enjoy a traditional meal. (a) <u>On the night before Thanksgiving</u>, our mother bakes a pumpkin pie, the traditional Thanksgiving dessert. (b) <u>In the morning</u>, she gets up early to prepare the other traditional dishes. (c) <u>First</u>, she makes dressing. (d) <u>Then</u> she stuffs the turkey with the dressing and puts the turkey into the oven to roast. (e) <u>After that</u>, she prepares the rest of the meal. She cooks all day long. (f) <u>About 3:00 in the afternoon</u>, the family sits down at the table. (g) <u>Before taking the first bite</u>, everyone around the table says one thing that they are thankful for. (h) <u>Finally</u>, we can begin to eat. We stuff ourselves just as full as Mother stuffed the turkey earlier in the day! (i) <u>Soon</u> we are all groaning because we have eaten too much. (j) <u>After dinner</u>, we collapse on the living room sofa and watch football games on TV. No one moves for at least two hours.

Fifteen Years

A girl's fifteenth birthday is a very special occasion in many Latin American countries and requires a lot of planning. (a) <u>Before the party</u>, the parents make many preparations. (b) <u>First</u>, they buy a special dress and order a bouquet of flowers for their daughter. They also plan a large meal for the guests and hire an orchestra. (c) <u>On the day of the party</u>, they decorate a big room where the party will be held. (d) <u>During the party</u>, there are many special traditions. (e) <u>At the beginning of the party</u>, the father and daughter enter the big salon accompanied by special music. (f) <u>Then</u> the father makes a speech, and the daughter gets some presents. (g) <u>After that</u>, everyone drinks champagne. (h) <u>Next</u>, the father and daughter dance a waltz, and the daughter and every boy dance one dance together. (i) <u>Then</u> all of the guests make a line to congratulate her. (j) <u>Finally</u>, all of the boys stand in a group because she will throw the bouquet, and the boy who catches it dances with her. (k) <u>Later</u>, everyone dances to different kinds of music until six o'clock in the morning.

C. 1. 7, 2, 5, 4, 3, 1, 6
   2. 7, 4, 1, 2, 6, 5, 3
   3. 6, 3, 4, 9, 7, 5, 1, 8, 2

Questions on the Model (page 29)
1. Time order.
2. Time order signals: Once upon a time, One day, During lunch, After a while.

Practice 2: Compound Sentences with *and, but, so,* and *or* (pages 30–32)

A. Sentence   2 – but (compound sentence)
                   3 – and (simple sentence)
                   4 – and (compound sentence)
                   5 – so (compound sentence)
                   7 – and (simple sentence)
                   9 – or (compound sentence)
                  10 – but (compound sentence)
                  11 – and (simple sentence)
                  12 – and (simple sentence)
                  13 – and (compound sentence)
                  14 – so (compound sentence)
                  15 – and (compound sentence)
                  16 – so (compound sentence)

B. Monsieur Seguin's Goat
    2. SS
    3. SS
    4. SS
    5. CS   . . . sad, and . . .
    6. SS
    7. SS
    8. CS   . . . rope, or . . .
    9. CS   . . . rope, but . . .
   10. SS
   11. CS   . . . decision, but . . .
   12. CS   . . . mountains, so . . .
   13. SS
   14. SS
   15. SS
   16. SS

C. Answers will vary. Sample answers:
2. She heard a noise and decided to go back to her enclosure.
3. She walked for a long time, but she couldn't find the road.
4. Finally, she became very tired and tried to rest, but her fear prevented her from sleeping.
5. Suddenly, a wolf appeared and looked at her hungrily.
6. She shouted for help, but no one heard her.
7. The wolf ate Blanchette, and the poor old man never saw his little goat again.
8. Blanchette wanted to be free, but freedom can be dangerous when we disobey.

D. Individual responses.

5

Practice 3: Commas (pages 33–34)

   A. 1. Daisy, Tomiko, Keiko, and Nina live near the college that they all attend.

         2. Tomiko and Keiko are from Japan, and Nina and Daisy are from Mexico.

         3. Nina and Keiko have the same birthday. Both girls were born on June 3 on different continents.

         4. Last week, the girls decided to have a joint birthday party, so they invited several friends for dinner.

         5. Nina wanted to cook Mexican food, but Keiko wanted to have Japanese food.

         6. Finally, they agreed on the menu.

         7. They served Japanese *tempura*, Mexican *arroz con pollo*, Chinese stir-fried vegetables, and American ice cream.

         8. First, Nina made the rice.

         9. Then Keiko cooked the *tempura*.

       10. After that, Tomiko prepared the vegetables.

       11. After dinner, Daisy served the dessert.

       12. The guests could choose chocolate ice cream or vanilla ice cream with chocolate sauce.

   B. Individual responses.

Chapter 3: Paragraph Structure

Questions on the Model (page 39)
1. A Hawaiian wedding
2. They are special occasions because of the mix of cultures.
3. Hawaiian weddings are multicultural.

Practice 1: Predicting Content from the Controlling Idea (page 40)
For discussion only. Possible responses:
1. Costs of rings, clothes, wedding place, gifts, party, food, flowers and other decorations, limousine, place to hold party (e.g. big hotel). Number of guests. Number of people in wedding party.
2. Couple + witnesses + marrying official, civil ceremony, simple rings, no party, no special clothes. Location at home or outdoors.
3. Examples of unusual places (beach, park, mountaintop, someone's garden, on a ship, etc.).

Practice 2: Topic Sentences (pages 40–42)
A. Check sentences 3, 6, 8, 9, 10, 12
   Too specific: 5, 7
   Too general: 4, 11
B. 1. c
   2. c
   3. c
C. Answers will vary. Possible answers:
   1. A teacher should have four qualifications.
   2. Food from other countries is very popular in the United States.
   3. People give different reasons for skipping breakfast.

Practice 3: Writing Supporting Sentences (pages 44–45)
Answers will vary. Possible answers:
1. b. A small car uses less gas.
   c. A small car is cheaper to maintain.
   d. Insurance for a small car may be cheaper.
2. b. Brush your teeth three times a day.
   c. Use dental floss daily.
   d. Visit your dentist twice a year.
3. b. Consider the abilities of everyone.
   c. Find out when everyone is available.
   d. Find out how much everyone can spend.

4. b. He/she is easy to get along with.
    c. You and he/she have similar interests.
    d. He/she is loyal.
5. b. Invite several friends to your house for a party.
    c. Forget your books and notes at school.
    d. Offer to help a friend with a big project such as painting his or her apartment.
6. b. It increases your knowledge in many subjects.
    c. You make friends with people in your field of study.

Practice 4: Signal Phrases for Examples (page 45)
1. For example, (or) For instance,
2. such as
3. For example, (or) For instance,

Practice 5: Supporting Sentences and Examples (page 46)

TOPIC SENTENCE

The mix of cultures in Hawaii makes weddings there very special occasions.

SUPPORTING POINT SENTENCE

Certainly, Hawaiian clothing, music, and other Hawaiian customs play a big role.

EXAMPLE

For example, the bride often wears a long white *holoku* (wedding dress), and the groom wears a long-sleeved white shirt and pants with a red sash around his waist.

EXAMPLE

Both the bride and the groom wear *leis*.

EXAMPLE

The bride's *lei* is traditionally made of white flowers such as *pikake* (jasmine), and the groom's is made of green *maile* leaves.

EXAMPLE

Another Hawaiian custom is the blowing of a conch shell three times to begin the ceremony.

EXAMPLE

Hawaiian music is played both during the ceremony and during the *luau* afterward.

SUPPORTING POINT SENTENCE

Other customs included in the festivities depend on the ethnic backgrounds of the couple.

EXAMPLE

For instance, there may be noisy firecrackers, a Chinese way of keeping bad spirits away.

EXAMPLE

There may be a display of Japanese *origami*, or there may a *pandango*, a Filipino custom.

EXAMPLE

During a *pandango,* the wedding guests tape money together and wrap it around the couple during their first dance together as husband and wife.

CONCLUDING SENTENCE

All in all, a Hawaiian wedding is truly a magical, multicultural event.

Practice 6: Concluding Sentences (pages 47–49)

    A. 1

    B. Answers will vary. Possible answers:

        1. These examples show that you can eat cheaply at the college cafeteria.

        2. In sum, watch children's television shows to learn a foreign language.

        3. In short, cell phones are everywhere.

Practice 7: Paragraph Structure (pages 49–50)

    Order of sentences: 3, 9, 4, 6, 1, 2, 7, 8, 5

TOPIC SENTENCE

Fast food is extremely popular in the United States, but it is not very good for you.

SUPPORTING POINT SENTENCE

First of all, most fast food is very high in calories.

EXAMPLE

For example, a 6-inch Pizza Hut Personal Pan pepperoni pizza has 660 calories, and a Big Mac from McDonald's has 560 calories.

SUPPORTING POINT SENTENCE

Second, a lot of the calories from fast food are from fat.

EXAMPLE

For instance, a portion of Nachos Supreme from Taco Bell contains 26 grams of fat, and a Big Mac contains 30 grams.

SUPPORTING POINT SENTENCE

Third, fast food items such as hamburgers and french fries contain high amounts of salt.

EXAMPLE

A typical meal at McDonald's contains as much as 1,370 milligrams of sodium.

SUPPORTING POINT SENTENCE

Finally, add a sugary soft drink to your fast-food meal, and you pound the last nail into the heart of any nutritionist.

CONCLUDING SENTENCE

In conclusion, stopping by a fast-food restaurant for a quick meal may be delicious and convenient, but it is definitely not a healthy way to eat.

Practice 8: Apostrophes (pages 53–54)

   A.   2. Carlos's roommate

          3. my country's flag

          4. the dancer's feet

          5. my child's school

          6. my children's school

          7. the boss's secretary

          8. the ladies' shoes

          9. the men's sweaters

        10. George Lucas's films

        11. the EU's president

   B.   2. Lance Armstrong's heart

          3. the color of her dress

          4. the teacher's desk

          5. the children's laughter

          6. the babies' mouths

          7. the mouth of the river

          8. the passengers' suitcases

   C. Individual responses.

Practice 9: Outlining (pages 55–56)

   A. **Animals in Captivity**

Animals living in modern zoos enjoy several advantages over animals in the wild.

      A. The first advantage is that zoo animals are separated from their natural predators.

         1. They are protected, so they live without risk of being attacked.

      B. Another advantage is that someone feeds them regularly, so they do not have to hunt for food.

         1. Also, they do not suffer times when food is hard to find.

      C. A third advantage of living in zoos is that veterinarians give animals regular checkups, and sick animals get prompt medical attention.

In conclusion, because all their needs are taken care of, most zoo animals are healthy and contented.

   B. **Bad Drivers**

There are three kinds of bad drivers you see on the streets and highways of almost any country.

      A. The first kind of bad driver is the wannabe Grand Prix racer.

         1. This kind of driver drives very aggressively.

         2. For example, he or she steps on the gas and roars away a millisecond before a traffic signal turns green.

         3. Driving in the passing lane and ignoring speed limits are normal for this kind of driver.

B. The second kind of bad driver is the modern multitasker.
   1. Modern multitaskers include drivers such as working mothers and overworked businessmen and women.
   2. They eat a sandwich, drink a cup of coffee, talk on their cell phone, and discipline the children fighting in the back seat while speeding down the highway at 65 mph.
C. The last kind is the cautious driver.
   1. The cautious driver drives v-e-r-y slowly and carefully.
   2. For instance, he or she drives no faster than 40 mph on highways and slows down to 30 on every curve.
   3. When making a turn, he or she almost comes to a full stop before inching around the corner.

In conclusion, bad drivers can be speedsters, "slowsters," or just inattentive, but you have to watch out for all of them!

Exercise: Summary Writing (page 59)

A. **Step 1** Answers will vary. Possible questions:
   1. Where is Marciela from?
   2. What is her educational history?
   3. What languages does she speak?
   4. Does she have work experience?
   5. What are her career goals?

   Step 2 Answers will vary. Sample summary:

   Marciela Perez is from El Salvador. She is a high school graduate and is taking English classes at City College. She speaks Spanish fluently, and she currently works in a factory. She wants to become a nurse practitioner.

B. Answers will vary.

Chapter 4: Descriptive Paragraphs

Questions on the Model (page 62)
1. The writer says that the house had a strange atmosphere.
2. The stairway was <u>dark</u>, <u>squeaking</u>, and <u>quite narrow</u>. Its steps were <u>high</u>.
3. He is looking up at her. First, he describes her whole appearance as elegant and middle-aged and her posture as leaning. He describes her eyes last.

Practice 1: Spatial Order Signals (page 63)
Spatial order words and phrases to add to the list:
> From the bottom of the stairway / beyond the darkness at the top of the stairway / against the wall / the first room beyond the stairs on the second floor / up the stairs / up the last step

Practice 2: Spatial Order Organization and Details (pages 63–64)
A. Answers will vary. Possible responses:
  1. Possible spatial order: counterclockwise from the doorway.
     b. A wet towel hangs over the doorknob.
     c. To the right of the door, makeup, hair curlers, and jewelry completely cover the top of the dresser.
  2. Possible spatial order: clockwise.
     a. In the front of the park is a children's play area. Children are swinging on the swings, sliding down the slide, and playing in the sand.
     b. To the left of the children's play area are benches for sitting.
     c. Behind the benches, boys are throwing Frisbees and playing soccer on the grass.
  3. Possible spatial order: near to far.
     a. The top of his workbench is completely free of clutter.
     b. Just above the workbench, he has a long shelf with jars full of different sizes of nails and screws.
     c. Above this shelf, there are hooks holding various small tools such as screwdrivers and pliers.
B. Individual responses.

Questions on the Model (page 65)
1. Behind my childhood home, there is a large piece of land that is surrounded by banana trees growing in wild disorder. The topic is "a large piece of land that is surrounded by banana trees." The controlling idea is "growing in wild disorder."
2. Yes: Now, whenever I hear the plop-plop-plop of raindrops on the roof of my small, tidy apartment in the city, I remember the beautiful, wild banana garden of my childhood.
3. Spatial order words and phrases to add to the list: Behind my childhood home, Surrounded by banana trees, Underneath the trees, In the center. There is a spatial pattern in the first part of the paragraph.
4. wild

Practice 3: Descriptive Details (pages 66–67)

A.

Sight		Smell	Sound	Touch	Taste
large	dark		cry out	moist	
wild	wide		melody	slick	
disorder	glossy		song		
crowds	small		plop-plop-plop		
green	tidy				
thick	beautiful				

B. Answers will vary. Possible responses:
2. crowds, crowded, people running, people hurrying, loudspeaker announcing arrivals of trains (subway), traffic rushing by (bus stop), horns honking, people pushing and shoving each other, smell of dampness (subway), smell of diesel exhaust (buses)
3. passengers rushing to their boarding gates, passengers waiting in long lines at counters/at security, people looking at the information boards, people waiting for their family or friends to exit from the passport control area, loudspeakers announcing arrivals and departures, loudspeakers making security announcements
4. ambulance sirens, loudspeakers paging doctors and other hospital personnel, people in the waiting area looking sad, stressed, sick, worried, anxious, medicinal hospital smell, empty paper cups, old magazines in waiting area, people talking in low voices
5. children laughing, dogs running in and out of the water, sunbathers sunning, waves lapping or crashing, birds flying low looking for fish, fisherman standing at water's edge casting their lines out, swimmers splashing, smell of salt, seaweed, shells lying on the sand

Practice 4: Unity (page 67)
1. Cross out sentences 5 and 6.
2. Cross out sentence 8.

Questions on the Model (page 68)
1. The ten-mile trail to Supai Village is hot and dusty. (Simple sentence.)
2. (2) You can hike the trail, or you can hire a guide to take you on horseback. (Compound sentence.)
   (3) Along the trail, you see only rock, sand, and an occasional lizard. (Simple sentence)

Practice 5: Compound Sentences with *yet, for,* and *nor* (pages 69–70)
A. Sentences 2, 7, 10, and 14 (*and*), 6 (*for*), 9 and 12 (*nor*)
B. 1. Muslims do not drink alcohol, nor do they eat pork.
   2. Some Christians do not work on Sunday, for Sunday is their day to worship.
   3. People who believe in the Hindu religion do not eat beef, for they believe that cows are sacred.

4. Muslim men are permitted to have four wives, yet few of them have more than one.

5. Buddhist monks do not marry, nor do they own property.

C. Responses will vary. Possible answers:

1. I have studied English for six years, yet I still can't speak it fluently.

2. Many children who watch television all day long don't learn how to read well, for they don't practice reading.

3. In some countries, women cannot vote, nor can they own property.

4. The United States is one of the richest countries in the world, yet there are many homeless people there.

5. Everyone should know at least two languages, for companies need bilingual employees.

D. Individual responses.

Practice 6: Varying Sentence Openings (page 71)

2. The resulting tsunami devastated the shores <u>of several countries</u> and killed nearly 250,000 people. (Not possible.)

3. Hundred-foot waves crashed <u>into homes and businesses</u> <u>in the towns</u> <u>near the coast</u>. (In the towns near the coast, hundred-foot waves crashed into homes and businesses.)

4. The giant earthquake came just three days <u>after a slightly smaller earthquake</u> <u>between Australia and New Zealand</u>. (Not possible.)

5. The energy released <u>by the earthquake</u> continued to be felt <u>for several months</u> <u>after the event</u>. (For several months after the event, the energy released by the earthquake continued to be felt.)

Skill Sharpeners Exercise 1: Commas (page 74)

1. Last Sunday, my friend and I were walking along the beach and spotted an interesting shell on top of the sand.

2. We stopped, knelt down, picked it up, and brushed the sand from its surface.

3. It was a disk about 3 inches in diameter with four V-shaped notches around its outer edge.

4. It was round, flat, and gray-white in color.

5. It was large for a sea shell, yet it weighed almost nothing.

6. I held it up to my nose and sniffed the salty smell of the ocean.

7. On the top side of the disk, Mother Nature had punched tiny holes in the shape of a flower with five petals.

8. The other side of the disk was very plain, for it had only one small hole in the center.

9. At first, we thought the shell was empty, but we were wrong.

10. We shook it, and a stream of sand fell out.

11. Later, we did a little research and learned that it wasn't a shell at all.

12. It was the skeleton of an ocean animal.

Skill Sharpeners Exercise 2: Summary Writing (page 74)

Answers will vary. Sample answers:

A child lived in a house with a strange atmosphere. He was standing at the bottom of a dark, narrow stairway. A woman was at top of the stairs. She stared at him with cold, unblinking eyes. He imagined that she was his mother, but now he knows that she was just a mannequin.

Chapter 5: Logical Division of Ideas

Questions on the Model (page 77)
1. The writer gives three reasons. The first (topic) sentence tells the number of reasons.
2. The first reason, The second reason, The third reason
3. The writer supports each reason wiith examples.

Practice 1: Recognizing Logical Division (page 79)
Responses will vary. Possible paragraph choices:
1. Practice 2A, Consistent Pronouns, page 80
2. Practice 2B, Paragraph 1 beginning "A marathon runner . . . ," page 80
3. Paragraph 2, "Men and Women Shoppers," page 82
4. Practice 3A, #2, Paragraph beginning "Today it is possible . . . ," page 85
5. Practice 4B, "Ways of Cooking Rice," page 90
6. Skill Sharpener Exercise 1, Unity, "Secrets of Good Ads," page 91

Practice 2: Consistent Pronouns (pages 80–81)
A. Some researchers believe that social animals such as <u>dogs</u> may have a sense of morality. That is, <u>dogs</u> know right from wrong. For example, <u>dogs</u> follow certain rules when <u>they</u> play together, and <u>they</u> exclude dogs that don't follow the rules. <u>Dogs'</u> sense of right and wrong also includes knowing how to behave correctly around humans. For example, <u>they</u> know who the pack leader (that is, the boss) in any family is. <u>They</u> also know that <u>they</u> are not allowed to eat the pack leader's food. If <u>they</u> steal a bite of food from Dad's dinner plate, <u>they</u> slink around the kitchen looking guilty because <u>they</u> know <u>they</u> have broken a rule. Other researchers say that fear of punishment, not guilt, is the reason for <u>dogs'</u> slinking behavior.

B. Paragraph 1:

<u>Marathon runners</u> must be strong not only in body but also in mind. <u>They have to</u> train for years to achieve the necessary endurance to compete in <u>their</u> sport. This requires great discipline and self-sacrifice. In addition, marathon runners have to train their minds in order to endure the long hours of solitary running. This, too, requires great discipline. In other words, <u>marathon runners</u> must be in top condition, both mentally and physically, if <u>they</u> want to run in marathons.

Paragraph 2:

Physicists are scientists who study the basic laws of nature and apply these laws to improve the world. They are concerned with scientific wonders as large as the universe or as small as an electron. <u>They are</u> problem solvers who <u>are</u> curious about the universe and who <u>are</u> interested in what gives it order and meaning.

Paragraph 3:

Many students feel that learning to write well is a useless, time-consuming task that has little to do with "real life"—that is, with their future occupations. Although this may be true if <u>they plan</u> to become an auto mechanic or a waitress, it is certainly not true if <u>they</u> plan to have a white-collar job. No matter what profession <u>they</u> enter—business, engineering, government, education—<u>they</u> will have to write.

Practice 3: Transition Signals (pages 85–87)

A. Responses may vary. Possible answers:
   1. a. First of all,   b. Second,   c. Then   d. Finally,
   2. a. Moreover,   b. In addition,   c. and   d. also
   3. a. For example,   b. such as   c. such as
B. 1. For example,
   2. . However,
   3. . Therefore, (or) Thus,
   4. . For instance,
   5. and, (or) so,
   6. . Then
   7. As a result,
   8. To sum up,

Practice 4: Editing for Sentence Errors (pages 89–90)

A. Answers may vary. Possible answers:
   3. Writing a paragraph is easy, but it takes practice.
   4. First, you write a topic sentence. Then you make an outline of the supporting sentences. (or) First, you write a topic sentence, and then you make an outline of the supporting sentences.
   6. College is not like high school. It is a lot harder.
   8. My parents did not finish high school. I was the first member of my family to graduate.
   9. In the old days, people did not have the opportunity to attend school. They had to work to help support the family. (or) In the old days, people did not have the opportunity to attend school, for they had to work to help support the family.
   10. Now parents want a better future for their children, so they encourage them to go to college and even help them achieve that goal. (or) Now parents want a better future for their children. They encourage them to go to college and even help them achieve that goal.

B. Responses may vary. Possible answers:
   3. Asian sticky rice is rinsed, soaked, cooked, and then steamed. The lid remains on the cooking pot during the entire cooking and steaming process.
   7. *Risotto* has a creamy texture. The individual grains have a chewy center.
   8. Persian rice is quite different, for it has a golden, crunchy crust. (or) Persian rice is quite different. It has a golden, crunchy crust.
   9. Thai people serve jasmine rice, and people in India enjoy basmati rice. Both kinds have a special perfume-like aroma.

Skill Sharpeners Exercise 1: Unity (page 91)

Cross out sentence 10.

Skill Sharpeners Exercise 2: Outlining (page 91)

Answers will vary. Possible outline:

A good ad has three characteristics.
   A. A good ad is simple.
      1. It lets pictures, not words, tell the story.
      2. All ads need some words, but a good ad has a powerful headline and only a small amount of text.
   B. A good ad is directed to a particular group of consumers.
      1. Ads for face creams are for older women.
      2. Ads for motorcycles are for unmarried young men.
   C. A good ad appeals to emotions.
      1. Women in the thirty-to-fifty age group want to look and feel younger.
      2. Teenagers want to feel popular.
In conclusion, good ads are simple, are directed at a specific group, and make an emotional connection.

Skill Sharpeners Exercise 3: Summary Writing (page 91)

Answers will vary. Possible summary:

There are three reasons I don't have a credit card. First, having a credit card makes it easy for me to buy things I can't afford. Second, charging purchases to a credit card leads to debt. Third, credit card contracts have "fine print" details that I may not understand at first.

Chapter 6: Process Paragraphs

Questions on the Model (page 95)
1. Topic sentence: Building a campfire with one match is easy if you follow these easy steps. The words *follow these easy steps* indicate that this paragraph will explain a process.
2. Six steps
3. It restates the topic sentence in different words.

Practice 1: Topic Sentences for Process Paragraphs (page 96)
Answers will vary.

Practice 2: Time Order Signals (pages 97–98)
A. Time order signals: The first step, Second, The next step, Next, Fifth, The last step, Soon
B. 1. The first step
   2. Second,
   3. The third step
   4. Finally,
   5. To sum up,
C. 1. 6, 8, 7, 2, 3, 4, 1, 5
   2. 2, 7, 9, 1, 4, 3, 6, 5, 8

Questions on the Model (page 100)
1. The verb is *squeeze*. It is a simple sentence.
2. Sentences 5, 6, 9, and 14 are simple sentences that are commands. (*Note*: Other sentences have clauses that are commands.)
3. It has two SV combinations: (you) hold – you count. The connecting word is *while*.

Practice 3: Complex Sentences (pages 102–103)
A. The three complex sentences with time clauses are 4, 8, and 11.
B. 2. Astronauts often feel seasick (when) they first experience weightlessness.
   3. Astronauts must exercise on special machines (while) they are orbiting Earth in their spacecraft.
   4. (When) the first Russian cosmonauts exited their spacecraft, they had to be carried (because) they could not walk.
   5. The students were silent (as) the teacher handed out the test.
   6. The students worked on the test problems (until) the teacher told them to stop.
   7. (As soon as) the teacher told them to stop writing, they put down their pencils.
   8. (After) the teacher collected the tests, she dismissed the class.
   9. (Before) she left, she promised to post their scores (where) students could view them.
   10. (Since) noise can change the heart rate and increase blood pressure, it is harmful to the body.
   11. Loud noise is especially harmful (as) it damages the ear drums.
   12. Rock musicians and construction workers can lose their hearing (because) they are exposed to loud noise over long periods of time.

C. 1 + b, 5 + a, 3 + c, 4 + e, 2 + d

The final paragraph may vary. Possible response:

During World War II, a British soldier got caught in a tree after he had parachuted into the jungles of Sumatra, Indonesia. While he hung helplessly in the trees, a wild monkey brought him bananas and other fruit every day. After twelve days had passed, the soldier finally succeeded in freeing himself. However, he still had a problem as he had no way to contact his comrades. The monkey continued to bring him fruit because it seemed to understand the problem and to want to help.

D. Individual responses.

Try It Out! (pages 103–104)

Answers will vary. Possible answers:

2. Because gorillas and chimpanzees are close relatives of humans, scientists have worked with them to study animal intelligence.
3. A young chimpanzee named Kanzi knows as much grammar as a two-and-a-half-year-old child, and a gorilla named Koko uses sign language to communicate with her trainer.
4. Most people believe that parrots can only imitate and (that they) don't understand what they are saying.
5. However, a parrot named Alex talks and seems to understand what he is saying.
6. He can answer questions about the color, shape, and size of a toy, and he can tell what it is made of.
7. Furthermore, Alex can also feel and communicate his feelings.
8. One day, when Alex made several mistakes in answering a question, he apologized and turned away.
9. Another time, Alex became sick, so his trainer had to leave him overnight in an animal hospital.
10. Because the hospital was a strange place, Alex didn't want to stay there alone.
11. When the trainer was going out the door, Alex cried out, "Come here. I love you. I'm sorry. Wanna go back."
12. Dolphins also show emotion during training.
13. When they are correct, they cry excitedly and race back to their trainer.
14. When they are wrong, they look sad and act depressed.
15. These few examples show that even animals with small brains are smart and have feelings.

Skill Sharpeners Exercise 1: Commas (page 105)

[1]Scrambled eggs are a quick and easy light meal. [2]You need two fresh eggs, milk, butter, salt, and pepper. [3]You also need a mixing bowl, a tablespoon, a fork, and a frying pan. [4]First, break the eggs into the bowl. [5]Then add about three tablespoons of milk, the salt, and the pepper. [6]Beat the mixture with a fork until it is well mixed. [7]Next, melt a small piece of butter in the frying pan over low heat. [8]Pour the egg mixture into the pan, and let it heat

21

through. ^{9}Then turn up the heat slightly. ^{10}As the eggs cook, push them around gently with the fork. ^{11}When the scrambled eggs are done to perfection, they should be light and fluffy. ^{12}In just a few minutes, you can sit down and enjoy your delicious meal.

Skill Sharpeners Exercise 2: Sentence Structure (page 106)

Sentences with errors and suggested corrections:

Sentence 2 (Comma splice) On the day of the ceremony, one of the groom's brothers goes to the bride's home with gifts. These gifts seal the union of the two families.

4 (Fragment) He is dressed in rich clothing and is wearing a special headdress.

11 (Fragment) He promises to make his wife happy . . .

14 (Run on) Musicians provide entertainment. Then a feast of traditional Indian food is served.

16 (Comma splice) The party may go on until midnight. Everyone is pretty tired at the end.

Skill Sharpeners Exercise 3: Unity (page 106)

Cross out sentences 3 and 14.

Chapter 7: Comparison/Contrast Paragraphs

Questions on the Models (page 111)
1. Paragraph 2
2. Paragraph 1
3. The left and right sides of your brain process information in different ways.
4. Shopping for an automobile
5. Following is a summary of their qualifications. (Sentence 2)
6. 4 similarities; 2 differences

Try It Out! (pages 112–113)

Main Topics	Alaska	Hawaii
accommodations	The quality of hotels – good Vary from basic to luxury	Wide range of excellent hotels and condos
climate	Temperature – perfect in the summer No humidity Seldom rains in the summer	Often rains in the summer Can be hot and humid in the summer
natural beauty	Chugach Mountains and Mount McKinley Glaciers – awesome	Volcano National Park and Waimea Canyon. Beaches – among the most beautiful in the world.

Outline and report will vary. Possible outline and report:

Outline

Alaska and Hawaii are two beautiful places to visit on a summer vacation.
- A. Accommodations – similar
  - 1. Alaska
    - a. Quality – good
    - b. Vary from basic to luxury
  - 2. Hawaii
    - a. Wide range of excellent hotels and condos
- B. Natural Beauty – similar
  - 1. Alaska
    - a. Chugach Mountains and Mount McKinley
    - b. Awesome glaciers

2. Hawaii
　　　　a. Volcano National Park and Waimea Canyon
　　　　b. Beautiful beaches
　C. Climate – different
　　1. Alaska
　　　　a. Perfect temperature in the summer
　　　　b. No humidity
　　　　c. Seldom rains
　　2. Hawaii
　　　　a. Often rains in summer
　　　　b. Can be hot and humid in summer

To sum up, for people who don't like heat and humidity, Alaska is the better choice, but for people who like beaches, Hawaii is the place to go.

Report

Alaska and Hawaii are two beautiful places to visit on your summer vacation. Both have good quality accommodations. In Alaska, accommodations vary from basic to luxury, and the quality of hotels is good. Hawaii has a wide range of excellent hotels and condos. Furthermore, both places attract visitors because of their natural beauty. Alaska has the Chugach Mountains and Mount McKinley, the highest mountain in North America, and it has many awesome glaciers. Hawaii's beaches are among the most beautiful in the world. Visitors can also visit Waimea Canyon and Volcano National Park. The summer climate is different in the two places. It often rains and can be hot and humid during the summer in Hawaii. In Alaska, the summer temperature is perfect, there is not humidity, and it seldom rains. To sum up, for people who don't like heat and humidity, Alaska is the better choice, but for people who like beaches, Hawaii is the place to go.

Questions on the Model (pages 114)

1. Topic sentence: Although U.S. English and U.K. English are mutually understandable languages, there are quite a few differences. It indicates that the paragraph will discuss mostly differences.
2. Comparison and contrast signals: Although, differences, difference, but, but, whereas, but, differences, like, in contrast, like, though
3. Other transition signals: One (difference), A second (area of difference), For example, Also, Finally, All in all
4. Logical division of ideas

Practice 1: Comparison Signals (pages 116–118)

A. similar, just as, equal, Similarly, the same (date), equally
B. Answers will vary. Possible answers:
　　2. Both overcrowded subways and <u>congested streets</u> are problems in Tokyo and New York City.
　　3. You can buy designer clothes not only in boutiques but also <u>in department stores</u>.
　　4. New Yorkers and Tokyoites can not only see a movie but can also <u>eat out</u> at any time.

5. In the summer, the weather in Tokyo and in New York is both hot and <u>humid</u>.
6. The Ginza and Fifth Avenue shopping districts have both fine jewelers and <u>famous designer boutiques</u>.

C. Answers will vary. Possible answers:
2. Like newspapers and magazines, radio and television need advertising to pay their costs.
3. The media reach millions of people around the world. Similarly, the Internet reaches people everywhere.
4. Just as most people read a daily newspaper, most people listen to the radio or watch television every day.
5. Printed and video pictures are equally powerful advertising media.

D. Answers will vary. Possible answers:
2. Knowing a second language is useful not only for travel but also for employment.
3. Like male students, female students participate in school sports.
4. High school students going to college have the same graduation requirements as high school students not going to college. (or) Graduation requirements are the same for high school students going to college and for high school students not going to college.
5. You can get a good education at both private and public universities. (or) Both private and public universities provide a good education.

Practice 2: Contrast Signals (pages 119–120)

A. on the other hand (appears twice), whereas (appears twice), In contrast, Although.

B. Answers will vary. Possible answers:
2. a. Fresh fruits and vegetables taste delicious, but canned ones are tasteless.
   b. Fresh fruits and vegetables taste delicious, whereas canned ones are tasteless.
   c. Fresh fruits and vegetables taste delicious. In contrast, canned ones are tasteless.
3. a. Eating well and exercising will keep you in good health, but exercising by itself will not.
   b. While eating well and exercising will keep you in good health, exercising by itself will not.
   c. Eating well and exercising will keep you in good health. However, exercising by itself will not.
4. a. A university has a graduate school, but a college usually does not.
   b. A university has a graduate school, while a college usually does not.
   c. A university has a graduate school. In contrast, a college usually does not.
5. a. Marco will go to college on a full scholarship, but Peter will have to work part time.
   b. Marco will go to college on a full scholarship, whereas Peter will have to work part time.
   c. Marco will go to college on a full scholarship. Peter, on the other hand, will have to work part time.

6. a. Medical care is free in Canada, but people must pay for it in the United States.
   b. Medical care is free in Canada, while people must pay for it in the United States.
   c. Medical care is free in Canada. In contrast, people must pay for it in the United States.

C. Answers will vary. Possible answers:
   2. Professor Rand's first exam was easy, yet 90 percent of the students failed it.
   3. Texting is a popular new way to communicate although it takes practice to do quickly.
   4. I work at a computer software company, whereas my grandparents do not know how to turn a computer on.
   5. The method of cooking rice in China is different from the method of cooking it in Italy.

Skill Sharpeners Exercise 1: Outlining (page 121)

Outlines may vary. Possible outline:

Two Varieties of English

Although U.S. English and British English are mutually understandable languages, there are quite a few differences.
   A. One difference is spelling.
      1. Some words are spelled one way in the United States but *spelt* another way in Great Britain.
      2. A person goes to a British *theatre* but to a U.S. theater.
      3. In U.S. schools, students theorize, analyze, and socialize, whereas British students *theorise, analyse*, and *socialise*.
   B. A second area of difference is vocabulary.
      1. For example, the word *college* describes two very different types of schools in the United States and Great Britain—university level in the United States and pre-university level in the Great Britain.
      2. Also, British university students live in *halls* on campus and in *flats* off campus, but U.S. students live in dormitories on campus and in apartments off campus.
   C. Finally, there are many differences in pronunciation.
      1. In Great Britain, the sound of *a* in the words *path, laugh, aunt, plant*, and *dance* is like the *a* in *father*.
      2. In the United States, in contrast, the *a* sound in the words is like the *a* in *cat*.
All in all, though there are many differences between the English spoken in the United States and the English spoken in the British Isles, we understand each other most of the time!

Skill Sharpeners Exercise 2: Summary Writing (page 121)
Summaries will vary. Possible summaries:

Right Brain/Left Brain

The two sides of your brain work differently. The left side processes information more logically, whereas the right side processes information more intuitively. A person who is more right-brained makes decisions after rational analysis. In contrast, a left-brained person bases decisions on feelings and sensory input.

Miller Medical Labs Memorandum

The two applicants for the receptionist position are equal in education, recommendations, and availability. They differ in experience and workplace preferences. JZ has had previous patient contact, whereas SW hasn't. Also, JZ wants to work with a team, while SW likes to work alone. I recommend JZ for this position.

Two Varieties of English

British and U.S. English are two varieties of the same language. They have some differences in spelling, vocabulary, and pronunciation.

Chapter 8: Definition Paragraphs

Questions on the Models (page 127)
1. Paragraph 1
   Topic: Underground Railroad
   Category or group: secret system
   Distinguishing characteristics: that helped slaves escape from slavery in the
      United States during the mid-1800s
   Paragraph 2
   Topic: Courage
   Category or group: quality
   Distinguishing characteristics: (of) being brave when you are facing something
      that is dangerous or that you fear
2. Paragraph 2 uses examples.
3. Paragraph 1 uses facts to answer *who, what, where, when,* and *how* questions.

Practice 1: Topic Sentences for Definition Paragraphs (page 128)
Answers will vary. Possible answers:
   2. An optimist is a person who has a positive attitude.
   3. A good friend is a person who is trustworthy.
   4. An ideal spouse is a woman (man) who is unselfish and caring.
   5. Chess is a game that requires concentration.

Practice 2: Commas with Appositives (page 131)
   A. Sentence 2: Iranian New Year (extra information appositive)
      Sentence 4: the language of Iran (extra information appositive)
      Sentence 12: large outdoor fires (extra information appositive)
   B. 3. *EI* Venus, the closest planet to Earth, is only 25 million miles away.
      4. *EI* The largest planet in the universe, Jupiter, is eleven times larger than Earth.
      5. *EI* Astronomers, scientists who study the stars, discovered a tenth planet in our solar
         system in 2005.
      6. *NI* The Moon is Earth's only natural satellite, but the planet Saturn has at least
         twenty-two satellites.
      7. *EI* Since the first artificial satellite, Sputnik 1, was launched by Russia in 1957,
         thousands of space probes, satellites, and telescopes have been sent into space.
      8. *EI* Also, millions of pieces of space junk, man-made garbage, zoom around Earth at
         speeds of up to 25,000 miles per hour.

Practice 3: Commas with Adjective Clauses (pages 132–133)

   2. *NI* Before Christianity existed, people in northern and central Europe worshipped a goddess <u>whom they called Eostre</u>. (modifies *goddess*)

   3. *EI* Eostre, <u>which means *east*</u>, was the goddess of spring. (modifies *Eostre*)

   4. *NI* Every spring people <u>who worshipped her</u> held a festival to give thanks for the return of the sun's warmth. (modifies *people*)

   5. *NI* They offered the goddess cakes <u>that they baked for the festival</u>. (modifies *cakes*)

   6. *EI* These cakes were very similar to hot cross buns, <u>which bakeries sell at Easter</u>. (modifies *hot cross buns*)

   7. *EI* Also, the custom of coloring eggs, <u>which families do at Easter</u>, came from ancient cultures. (modifies *the custom of coloring eggs*)

   8. *EI* Even the popular Easter Bunny, <u>who brings chocolate eggs and other candy to children on Easter Sunday</u>, has pagan roots. (modifies *Easter bunny*)

Practice 4: Adjective Clauses with Subject Pronouns (pages 134–135)

   A. 2. Judaism, which is the oldest major religion in the world, has very strict rules about food.

      3. Christians who practice fasting do not eat certain foods during the six weeks before Easter.

      4. People who practice the Hindu religion cannot eat beef.

      5. Muslims and Jews cannot eat pork, which is considered unclean.

      6. Muslims cannot eat or drink at all in the daytime during Ramadan, which is a holy month of fasting.

   B. 2. Gautama Siddhartha, who started Buddhism, was born about 500 years before Jesus.

      3. Christianity was started by Jesus, who was born about 500 years before Mohammed.

      4. Mohammed founded Islam, which is the second largest religion in the world.

      5. A religion that has only one God is monotheistic.

      6. The Hindu and Shinto religions, which have many gods, are polytheistic.

Practice 5: Adjective Clauses with Object Pronouns (pages 136–137)

   A. 1. People in Thailand have a festival that they call *Loy Krathong*, "Festival of the Floating Leaf Cups."

      2. The Thais float little boats that they have made out of banana leaves, lotus, or paper down a river in the evening.

      3. The boats, which they have decorated with lighted candles, incense, coins, and flowers, float down the river in the moonlight.

   B. 1. On the first day of *Pongal*, families gather in the kitchen and boil a pot of new rice, which they cook in milk.

      2. Then they offer some of the sweet rice to the sun god, whom they thank for ripening the rice crop.

3. The second day of *Pongal* is for the rain, which they thank for helping the rice to grow.
4. A traditional *Pongal* gift is a clay horse, which they paint in bright colors.
5. On the third day of *Pongal*, the farmers honor their cattle, which they decorate with flowers and coins.

Practice 6: Clauses with *When* (page 138)
1. Were you alive on July 20, 1969, when the first human walked on the moon?
2. Every mother remembers the wonderful day when her first child was born.
3. *Tet* is a special time when Vietnamese people celebrate the lunar new year.

Practice 7: Adjective Clauses (pages 139–140)
Answers will vary. Possible answers:
- A. 2. A coach is a person who teaches a sport.
  3. Travel agents are people who help people plan trips.
  4. MP3 players are devices that record and play back music.
  5. A fork is a utensil that Western people use for eating.
  6. Chopsticks are utensils that Asian people use for eating.
  7. Valentine's Day is a day when friends and lovers exchange cards and gifts.
- B. A blog, which is an abbreviation of weblog, is an online diary that a person posts on a webpage.

  An airhead is a person who is not very intelligent and is usually silly.

  A couch potato is a person who sits on a sofa all day, usually watching television.

  A no-brainer is something that requires no thought.

  A nutcase is a person who is strange or crazy.

  A potluck dinner is a dinner which everyone brings food to.

  A sitting duck is a person who is an easy target or victim.

  A geek is a person who is very knowledgeable about science and technology but who is socially unskilled.

  A slam dunk is something that is very easy to do.

  A dot com is a company that operates its business primarily on the Internet using a URL that ends in ".com".

  A tightwad is a person who doesn't like to spend money.

  An emoticon is a face that shows emotion that you can make on a computer with punctuation marks. Examples: :-) or :-(

Try It Out! (pages 140–141)
Answers will vary. Possible answers:
2. A modern Thanksgiving is similar in many ways to the first Thanksgiving, which took place almost four hundred years ago in the English colony of Massachusetts.
3. In 1620, the Pilgrims, who were a religious group from England, arrived in Plymouth, Massachusetts.

4. The Pilgrims came to the New World because their religion was different from the main religion in England.
5. The Pilgrims' first winter was very hard, and almost half the group died.
6. They died of hunger, cold, and disease.
7. During the next year, the Wampanoag, who were a tribe of Native Americans in Massachusetts, helped them.
8. The Wampanoag taught the newcomers how to hunt, grow corn, and survive in the New World.
9. When the next winter came, the Pilgrims had enough food.
10. Because they were grateful, they had a feast to give thanks.
11. They shared food and friendship with the Wampanoag, whom they invited to the feast.
12. A modern Thanksgiving is similar in spirit to the first Thanksgiving, but the food is probably different.
13. Today Americans eat turkey, but the Pilgrims and Wampanoag probably ate deer.

Skill Sharpeners Exercise 1: Scrambled Definition Paragraph (page 142)

A. Answers will vary. Possible order:

6, 4, 7, 2, 3, 1, 5

B. Adjective clauses:

Sentence 1 – that could be mass produced

Sentence 6 – who designed simple "glass box" buildings and changed the look of cities worldwide

Sentence 7 – that greatly changed building design

Appositive:

Sentence 7 – a style that greatly changed building design

Skill Sharpeners Exercise 2: Unity (page 143)

Cross out sentence 8.

Chapter 9: Essay Organization

Questions on the Model (page 150)
1. Three styles are discussed: reggae, punk, and rap.
2. There are three body paragraphs. Their topics and topic sentences are as follows:
   Body paragraph 1: reggae music. <u>One successful style of popular music is reggae, which was born on the Caribbean island of Jamaica in the 1960s and spread throughout the world in the 1970s.</u>
   Body paragraph 2: punk music. <u>A second successful style of popular music is punk.</u>
   Body paragraph 3: rap music. <u>A third successful style of popular music is rap, which is also called *hip-hop*.</u>
3. Transition words and phrases:
   Introducing body paragraph 1: One
   Introducing body paragraph 2: A second
   Introducing body paragraph 3: A third
4. Logical division of ideas
5. Possible answers: how it started, where it started, when it started, how it is played, what its characteristics and/or themes are, who the best-known musicians or groups are

Practice 1: The Introductory Paragraph (page 151)
1. 3, 4, 5, 2, 1
2. 4, 1, 3, 2
3. 3, 1, 2

Practice 2: Topic Sentences for Body Paragraphs (page 152)
Answers will vary. Possible answers:
1. A. First of all, young people who live at home save money on rent, utilities, and food.
   B. Second, they don't have to cook, clean house, or do laundry.
   C. Third, they have the emotional support of their families.

or

   A. They can come and go whenever they want.
   B. They can make their own decisions.
   C. They don't have to follow their parents' rules.
2. Individual responses.
3. A. Cell phones allow us to talk to or text message anyone, anywhere, and at any time.
   B. Computers allow us to e-mail and instant message.
   C. BlackBerries let us send and receive e-mail from anywhere.
4. Individual responses.

Practice 3: Concluding Paragraphs (pages 153–156)

1. (1)
2. (2)
3. (2)
4. (1)

Practice 4: Transitions Between Paragraphs (pages 157–159)

Answers will vary. Possible answers:

Paragraph 3: *Besides improving communication*, personal computers are changing the way we do business.

Paragraph 4: *Moreover*, telecommuting—working at home instead of going to the office—has become a choice for thousands of business people.

Paragraph 5: *In addition to changing the way we communicate and do business*, personal computers have changed to world of education.

Paragraph 6: *On the other hand*, not everyone agrees that computers are good for education.

Paragraph 7: *Furthermore*, computers have caused problems for society.

Paragraph 8: *To conclude*, the computer age has arrived, and it has changed our lives.

Practice 5: Outlining an Essay (pages 160–162)

Answers will vary. Possible outline:

I. Introduction

Thesis Statement: Three of the more successful styles are reggae, punk, and rap.

II. Body

A. One successful style of popular music is reggae.

1. Born on the Caribbean island of Jamaica in the 1960s
   a. Spread throughout the world in the 1970s
2. Developed from mento
   a. Changed into ska by adding a hesitation beat
   b. Later changed into reggae
3. Special sound comes from reversing roles of instruments
   a. Guitar plays rhythm and bass plays melody.
4. Important influence—Rastafarian cult
   a. unusual sound mixes
   b. extra-slow tempos
   c. strange lyrics
   d. mystical-political themes
5. Bob Marley—best known reggae musician
   a. Groups—Toots & The Maytals, UB40, Soldier of Jah Army
6. Reggae has influenced later styles

B. A second successful style of popular music is punk.
   1. Began in the 1970s as a reaction against previous forms of rock
      a. Punks felt that rock no longer represented counterculture.
   2. With clothing and hairstyles, punks intended to shock society.
      a. Punk look: hair, makeup, clothing, piercings, jewelry
   3. On-stage behavior: aggressive and provocative
      a. Fans—fighting
   4. Punk music is simple.
      a. Often just 3 chords
      b. Short songs
      c. Songs are anti-government, anti-authority, anti-conformity
   5. First bands: Sex Pistols, Clash, Ramones
   6. Punk has evolved into other styles.
      a. Hardcore punk: Dead Kennedys, Black Flag
      b. Emo: Fall Out Boy
      c. Pop punk: Green Day
C. A third successful style of popular music is rap.
   1. Also known as hip-hop
   2. Form of dance music—singers speak in rhythm and rhyme
   3. Originated in Africa
      a. Traveled to the U.S. via Jamaica—"toasting"
      b. In the U.S., first appeared in discos in NYC black neighborhoods mid-1970s
      c. Disco DJs + rappers played songs for dancers at parties
      d. Rapper kept the beat by hand clapping while DJ changed records.
      e. Rappers added lyrics, slogans, rhymes, call-and-response.
   4. Early themes: dancing, partying, romance
      a. Politics—theme in 1980s and 1990s
   5. Most rappers are young black males.
      a. Female rapper—Queen Latifah
      b. White rappers: Beastie Boys and Eminem
III. Conclusion

Popular music changes constantly. New styles are born, grow, change, and produce offshoots, which in turn grow, change, and produce offshoots. Some styles enjoy lasting popularity, but others disappear rather quickly. However, all contribute to the power and excitement of popular music in our time.

Practice 6: Grouping Ideas Logically (pages 163–164)

A. Produce: apples, carrots, oranges, lettuce, potatoes, tomatoes
   Dairy Products: milk, cheese, eggs
   Meat: hamburger, pork chops, steak
   Baked Goods: bread, pie, cookies, cake, doughnuts
   Personal Care/Health Products: aspirin, vitamins, shampoo, toothpaste

B. Answers will vary. Possible groups/categories:
   1. a. Individual sports: fishing, hiking, ice skating, jogging, mountain climbing, scuba diving, skateboarding, waterskiing, windsurfing
      b. Team sports: baseball, basketball, ice hockey, soccer, volleyball
      c. Both team and individual: badminton, bobsledding, bowling, diving, golf, gymnastics, skiing, swimming, table tennis. tennis
   2. a. Summer sports
      b. Winter sports
   3. a. Indoor sports
      b. Outdoor sports
   4. a. Water sports
      b. Ball sports
   5. a. Sports that need equipment
      b. Sports that don't need equipment
C. Responses will vary. Possible groups/categories:
   1. Good lies
      Diplomatic lies/social lies/polite lies
         Friend who failed an important exam
         Friend who didn't get a job he/she wanted
      Lying to avoid hurting someone's feeling
         Bad haircut
         Clothes that don't fit/don't look good/out of style
   2. Bad lies
      Lies to get out of trouble
         Children who do something bad
            Broken window
            Stole a cookies
      Lies that hurt someone's feelings
      Malicious lies that harm another person
      Lies to avoid punishment
         Lying to a police officer when caught speeding
      Lies to save face
      Lying on a job application

Practice 7: Outlining Body Paragraphs (page 164)
   Answers will vary.

Skill Sharpeners Exercise: Sentence Structure Review (pages 165–166)
Answers may vary. Possible corrections (underlined):

Left-Handedness

Do you know anyone who is left-handed? You probably do, <u>for</u> about 10 percent of the population uses their left rather than their right hand for writing and other tasks. Although many athletes, musicians, artists, and world leaders are left-handed, being left-handed certainly has a few disadvantages in a world designed by and for right-handed people.

Social situations can provide opportunities for left-handed people to feel clumsy. <u>First of all, handshakes are a small problem</u>. Right-handed people offer their right hands and expect to grasp the right hand of the other person. The instinct of left-handers, however, is to extend their left <u>hand. They</u> have to train themselves to extend their right. Another social opportunity for awkwardness occurs at the dinner table. Left-handed diners constantly bump elbows with a right-handed <u>person unless</u> they sit at the far end of the table with no one on their left. What's worse, left-handers have to concentrate in order to avoid grabbing and drinking from the wrong glass.

Left-handed people can face inconveniences at school, too. Consider the chairs in classrooms with little fold-up desktops for taking notes. Most of them are made for right-handers. Left-handers have to write with their left elbow hanging in mid<u>-air or else</u> turn themselves around almost 180° in order to lay their notebook on the desk. Furthermore, when lefties write in a three-ring binder or spiral <u>notebook, the</u> rings get in the way of their hands when they write on the front side of a page. Finally, left-handers write from left to <u>right, so</u> their hand smears the fresh ink across the page.

Last but not least are the many inventions of the modern <u>world that</u> make life convenient for right-handers but inconvenient for lefties. These include scissors, can openers, corkscrews, automobile gear shifts, cameras, and computer keyboards.

In sum, in a world organized for right-handers, left-handed people must confront and overcome challenges every day.

Practice 8: Summarizing an Essay (page 167)
Answers will vary. Possible summaries:

Styles of Popular Music

Reggae, punk, and rap are three successful styles of popular music. Reggae started in Jamaica. It developed from Afro-Caribbean music. Its unusual sound comes from switching the roles of the guitar and bass and from adding a hesitation beat. Reggae was influenced by the Rastafarians. Punk started because punks felt that rock music had lost its image of rebellion. Punk music is simple, and punks show their rejection of society by their weird hair, bizarre clothing, and confrontational behavior. Rap is dance music. Rappers speak in rhythm rather than sing the words of songs. Originally, its songs were about having fun, love, and later, about politics. Most rappers are young black males.

Left-Handedness

A person who is left-handed sometimes faces awkward situations. One situation is shaking hands. Most people offer their right hands, so a left-handed person has to consciously extend his or her right hand. Left-handed people also eat with their left hands, so they often bump elbows with right-handers at the dinner table, and they must remember not to reach for the drinking glass or coffee cup on their left. Furthermore, writing is difficult on school desks with fold-up desktops and in three-ring binders and spiral notebooks. Finally, many modern inventions such as computer keyboards, scissors, and cameras can be awkward for lefties to operate.

Chapter 10: Opinion Essays

Questions on the Model (page 171)

1. Although many people feel that doctors must do everything possible to keep their patients alive, I believe that euthanasia should be legal for three reasons. The reader can expect three body paragraphs.

2. There are three body paragraphs.
   Topic sentences:
   Body paragraph 1: The (first and most important) reason to support euthanasia is that some patients who have no chance to recover do not wish to be kept alive on machines.
   Body paragraph 2: A (second) reason to support euthanasia is that medical costs in the United States are very high.
   Body paragraph 3: The (final) reason to support legalizing euthanasia is that the family suffers.

3. The first body paragraph has a concluding sentence: Clearly, when there is absolutely no hope of recovery, society should allow a person in Terri Schiavo's condition to die if that is his or her wish.

4. The conclusion summarizes the three reasons.

Practice 1: Thesis Statements for Opinion Essays (pages 171–172)

A. Although

B. but

C. Answers will vary. Sample answers:

2. Many people believe that women should not serve in the military, but I believe that they should for two main reasons.

3. Society often ignores steroid use by well-known professional athletes because of the athletes' popularity. However, I believe these athletes should suffer the same punishment that ordinary citizens suffer for using illegal drugs.

4. Although professional athletes undoubtedly feel that they deserve their million-dollar salaries, I feel their high salaries are ruining sports.

5. Some people are in favor of drug testing for high school athletes, but I feel that this is a bad idea for several reasons.

6. Some people feel that the United States needs more laws to control the sale and ownership of guns. However, I feel that gun control laws are wrong for three reasons.

Practice 2: Developing Reasons (page 173)

Answers will vary depending on the topics chosen.

Practice 3: Punctuating Quotations (pages 175–176)

1. Dr. T. Berry Brazelton said, "The average child today spends more time in front of a TV set than she does studying in school or talking with her parents."

2. "As a result," he added, "children often learn more about the world and about values from television than from their families."
3. "A majority of child characters on ABC, NBC, CBS, and Fox programs tend to engage in antisocial behavior such as lying or physical aggression," reported Damon Ho, president of Parents for Responsible Programming.
4. Advice columnist Abigail van Buren wrote in a recent column, "The television set may provide some people with the only human voice they hear for days."
5. "It provides news and entertainment for millions of people who cannot leave the comfort, privacy, and safety of their homes," she continued.
6. "Not everyone can attend college in a traditional way," says Greenhills College professor Caroline Gibbs, "so we televise courses that students can view on their TV sets at home."

Practice 4: Supporting Details (page 176)
1. Example
2. Statistics
3. Example and quotation

Skill Sharpeners Exercise 1: Outlining (pages 178–179)
Outlines will vary. Sample outline:

Thesis Statement:	Although many people feel that doctors must do everything possible to keep their patients alive, I believe that euthanasia should be legal for three reasons.
	A. The first and most important reason to support euthanasia is that some patients who have no chance to recover do not wish to be kept alive on machines.
Example	1. Terry Schiavo's story
	B. Medical costs are very high.
Statistic	1. Daily hospital room charges average $5,000.
Statistic	2. A nursing home charges $4,500 per month.
	C. The family suffers.
Example	1. My cousin's story
Quotation	2. "Of course I am sad, but since we all knew he would eventually die, it might have been better if it had happened right when he had the accident. These past eight years have been hard."
Conclusion:	To summarize, patients who are either terminally ill or who are in an irreversible coma often wish to die. Their care is a financial, physical, and emotional burden for their families. Therefore, families should have the right to ask doctors to turn off life-support machines or to remove feeding tubes.

Skill Sharpeners Exercise 2: Summarizing an Essay (page 179)
Responses will vary. Sample summary:

There are three reasons for making euthanasia legal. First, a person who is in a permanent coma or who has a terminal disease and wishes not to be kept alive on machines should be allowed to die. Second, the financial cost of keeping a person in a hospital or nursing home can cause financial ruin for their families. Third, the physical and emotional burden on families is very great.